THE AMERICAN FLAG

THE American FLAG

BY ANN ARMBRUSTER

Franklin Watts
New York • London • Toronto • Sydney
A First Book   1991

Cover photograph courtesy of Roberto Fuenmayor

Photographs copyright © : FPG International: pp. 2 (Jim Howard), 48 (P. Karas);
Pictorial Parade: p. 8 (Vals); UPI/Bettmann Newsphotos: pp. 35, 52, 53; Flag
Research Center, Winchester, Ma.: pp. 10, 18 bottom, 32; Gamma-Liaison Inc.: pp.
11 (Luc Novovitch), 36 (Brent Clingman); The Bettmann Archive: pp. 14, 16
bottom, 18 top; Culver Pictures, Inc.: pp. 16 top, 23, 26 bottom, 43 right; The
Smithsonian Institution: p. 24; Wide World Photos: p. 26 top; Historical Pictures
Service, Chicago: pp. 31, 34 top, 43 left; VFW Magazine: p. 34 bottom;
Art Resource Inc., N.Y.: pp. 40, 42; New York Public Library,
Picture Collection: p. 45.

Library of Congress Cataloging-in-Publication Data

Armbruster, Ann.
    The American Flag / Ann Armbruster.
        p.   cm. — (A First book)
    Includes bibliographical references and index.
    Summary: Discusses the history of the American flag, its
symbolism, its role during various wars, its place as a motif in
art, flag facts, and etiquette.
    ISBN 0-531-20045-0
    1. Flags—United States—History—Juvenile literature.
[1. Flags—History.] I. Title. II. Series
CR113.A87   1991
929.9′2′0973—dc20   91-3771 CIP AC

CONTENTS

THE AMERICAN FLAG

*Many cities and
towns have Fourth
of July parades
each year.*

INTRODUCTION

When you watch a Fourth of July parade, you hear the beat of the drums and then, as the parade approaches, you see the flag flying in the breeze. You might feel very emotional as people cheer and salute the flag as it passes. A flag can produce deep reactions in the people who view it. To some people it may represent loyalty to their country or dedication to some cause; to others the flag is the symbol of all they believe in, a constant reminder of who they are.

The importance of a flag lies in the message it carries. It is a means of communication from one group of people to another. Flags of specific colors are often used as signals: white for surrender, red for warning, yellow for sickness and quarantine, and black for death and mourning.

Although the origins of the earliest flags are unknown, flaglike symbols have been used since the beginning of recorded history. The ancient Egyptians used fans of feathers, which were symbols of their Pharaohs, or rulers, while the Chinese may have

*Above: this colorful dragon flag was
used in China between 1890 and 1912.*

*Right: an enthusiastic crowd
proudly displays the
Stars and Stripes.*

been the first to make flags of woven cloth. Some of the first flags were animal skins or carved images of birds attached to poles by different tribes.

Whatever its color or shape, a nation's flag is a visual symbol of its heritage. Citizens may salute it, may show contempt for it, or may ignore it, but the flag represents the history of their country.

THE STARS AND STRIPES FOREVER

Most of us celebrate a birthday, a day that marks the beginning of our lives. June 14, Flag Day, celebrates the birthday of the American flag, which now displays fifty stars, one for each state in the Union. The original Stars and Stripes contained only thirteen stars, which represented the thirteen original states of our country. You can see how the flag reflects the enormous growth and development of the United States.

Since no accurate records were kept concerning its early history, numerous legends surround our flag's origin. In recent years, modern researchers have disproved some of the stories, carefully sifting the "flag myths" from true historical facts.

★ Early Flags in America ★

No one knows exactly who brought the first flags to America. Some historians claim it was the Vikings, who arrived in the

The thirteen stars in this early flag represent the thirteen original states.

The Vikings may have flown a flag like the one in this engraving when they sailed to America in the tenth and eleventh centuries.

tenth and eleventh centuries, bearing their flag, a black raven on a white background. During the sixteenth and seventeenth centuries, the flags of France, Spain, the Netherlands, and especially Great Britain played prominent roles in pre-revolutionary America. The Stars and Stripes reflects the cultural influence of the explorers and settlers who came here to found a new land.

★ Colonial Flags ★

As dissent grew between Great Britain and the American colonies, numerous flags arose out of the turmoil. These flags often displayed the feelings people had for their region or the political events that were affecting them.

The Rattlesnake Emblem

The rattlesnake was the favorite animal emblem of the rebellious Americans. Pictures of a dismembered rattlesnake were published in Benjamin Franklin's newspaper, *The Pennsylvania Gazette*, in 1751, to remind local citizens of the dangers of disunity. The snake was cut into pieces and each section marked with the name of a colony, followed by the motto JOIN OR DIE.

The Pine Tree Emblem

The pine tree, representative of New England, was another popular symbol. One of the most famous flags with this design was the flag flown at Bunker Hill in June of 1775. The Pine Tree flag might have become the emblem of the new country, but many people felt it was too closely associated with the New England colonies.

JOIN or DIE

The rattlesnake on this flag from about 1751 reminded the colonies to "unite and conquer."

GROUP OF COLONIAL FLAGS No. 2.
COPYRIGHT 1898, BY ADDIE G. WEAVER

Several different flags were used during the Revolution, including those shown here.

The Continental Colors

This flag was the first step in the evolution of the Stars and Stripes. It combined the British Union Jack and the thirteen red and white stripes representing the American colonies. In this way, Americans demonstrated that the thirteen colonies were still loyal to the king but opposed to certain acts of Parliament.

On January 1, 1776, in celebration of the new Continental Army, the Continental Colors was raised for the first time—on Prospect Hill in Somerville, Massachusetts. This site was near George Washington's encampment at Cambridge, Massachusetts. Washington later wrote that "We had hoisted the Union Flag in compliment to the United Colonies."

★ The First Stars and Stripes (1777–1795) ★

After the signing of the Declaration of Independence on July 4, 1776, Americans recognized the need for a new flag to represent this new country. On June 14, 1777, the Continental Congress finally passed the Flag Resolution: "Resolved that the Flag of the United States be 13 stripes alternate red and white: that the union [the upper left section] be 13 stars, white in a blue field, representing a new constellation."

So, the first Stars and Stripes was created by making one simple change in the Continental Colors. The crosses of St. George and St. Andrew were replaced with a "new constellation" of American stars.

Francis Hopkinson

Many controversial claims have been made concerning the designer of our first Stars and Stripes. In 1780, Francis Hopkinson,

a delegate to the Continental Congress and a signer of the Declaration of Independence, presented a bill to Congress for "services rendered," which included designs for a flag. His efforts were acknowledged, but he was not paid because Congress believed that other people had been involved in the design.

★ The Growth of the Stars and Stripes ★

In 1795, after Vermont and Kentucky were admitted to the union, Congress decided that the flag should have fifteen stars and fifteen stripes (one star and one stripe for each state). With the continued growth of the country in the nineteenth century, this design became impractical.

In 1818, a new Flag Act was passed which required that the number of stripes be reduced to the original thirteen and the number of stars be determined by the number of states. This resolution remains as our basic flag legislation. But it wasn't until 1912 that the relative proportions of the flag were officially determined.

Top: the Grand Union Flag was first flown by John Paul Jones on his flagship in December 1775. Bottom: a corner of the British Union Jack formed part of the design of the Grand Union Flag.

In the following chart you can trace the changes in the flag as new states were added.

NUMBER OF STARS IN FLAG	STATES AND DATE ADMITTED TO UNION
13	The original thirteen founding states: Delaware, Pennsylvania, New Jersey, Georgia, Connecticut, Massachusetts, Maryland, South Carolina, New Hampshire, Virginia, New York, North Carolina, Rhode Island
15	Vermont (1791), Kentucky (1792)
20	Tennessee (1796), Ohio (1803), Louisiana (1812), Indiana (1816), Mississippi (1817)
21	Illinois (1818)
23	Alabama (1819), Maine (1820)
24	Missouri (1821)
25	Arkansas (1836)
26	Michigan (1837)
27	Florida (1845)
28	Texas (1845)

29	Iowa (1846)
30	Wisconsin (1848)
31	California (1850)
32	Minnesota (1858)
33	Oregon (1859)
34	Kansas (1861)
35	West Virginia (1863)
36	Nevada (1864)
37	Nebraska (1867)
38	Colorado (1876)
43	North Dakota (1889), South Dakota (1889), Montana (1889), Washington (1889), Idaho (1890)
44	Wyoming (1890)
45	Utah (1896)
46	Oklahoma (1907)
48	New Mexico (1912), Arizona (1912)
49	Alaska (1959)
50	Hawaii (1959)

2
THE FLAG
MAKERS

★ The Betsy Ross Legend ★

Of all the legends about the flag, the Betsy Ross story is the most persistent. As the story goes, in 1776 Betsy Ross, a Philadelphia seamstress, was visited by George Washington and a congressional committee, who showed her a sketch of a proposed new flag. Suggesting some alterations, the seamstress supposedly then sewed a flag of wool bunting with thirteen red and white stripes and thirteen stars set in a circle.

The source of this story was a speech given by Mrs. Ross's grandson, William J. Canby, in 1870. There is no proof that these claims are true, but over the years Betsy Ross has become a folk heroine. Her shop at 239 Arch Street in Philadelphia is visited each year by thousands of people.

Many have heard the story that Betsy Ross made the first American flag, but it is not certain the story is true. This painting shows her at work on the flag in Philadelphia.

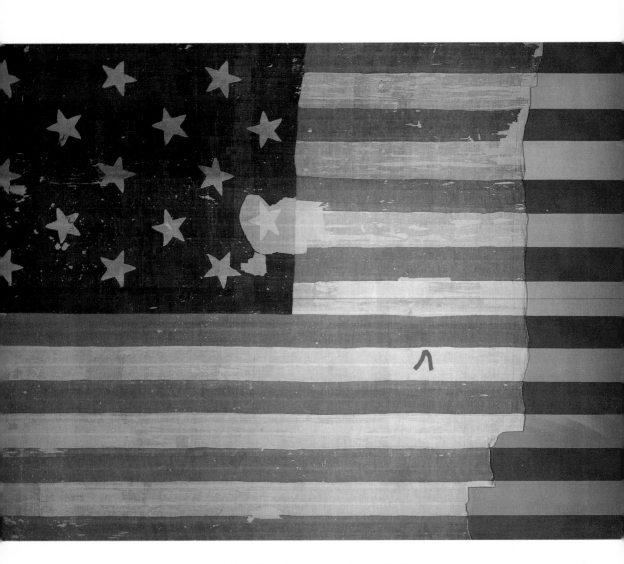

This flag flew over Fort McHenry during the War of 1812. It can be seen at the Smithsonian Institution in Washington, D.C.

The original Star-Spangled Banner, which flew over Fort Mc-Henry in Baltimore during the War of 1812, was made by a Baltimore seamstress, Mary Young Pickersgill, and her daughter Caroline for the sum of $405.90. At that time, there were no government funds available to pay for the cost of the flag so Colonel George Armistead, commander of the fort, paid for it personally.

This flag of fifteen stars and fifteen stripes was the garrison flag of Fort McHenry. At that time it was the largest flag in the world, weighing 90 pounds (40.8 kg) and measuring 42 feet (12.8 m) by 30 feet (9.1 m).

In 1914, Amelia Fowler of Boston and a group of expert needlewomen sewed a million and a half six-sided stitches to secure the battered Fort McHenry flag to a linen background in order to preserve it for future generations. This work was done in the hall of the Smithsonian Institution in Washington, D.C., where the flag is now displayed.

★ Today's Flag Makers ★

Today's flag makers use a variety of construction methods. Flags are printed, appliquéd, and embroidered on natural or synthetic materials especially made for flags. Huge machines produce hundreds of star fields at the same time other machines combine strips of red and white fabric to form the stripes.

A prime concern of the manufacturers is colorfastness, which must be insured for the duration of the flag. This is achieved by special curing, washing, and drying operations.

While flag materials have changed, so have the colors. Many American flags are made from synthetic fibers, and the traditional red, white, and blue in these flags are brighter than the colors in wool or cotton bunting flags.

The largest free-flying United States flag is made by Annin and Company, one of the world's largest flag manufacturers. This flag, which measures 60 feet (18.3 m) by 90 feet (27.4 m), flies at the New Jersey end of the George Washington Bridge on patriotic holidays. Stored in the superstructure of the bridge, the 500-pound (227-kg) flag is raised and lowered by an intricate rigging device.

*Top: a worker in a modern flag-making
plant uses strong thread and a
heavy-duty sewing machine
to assemble flags.
Bottom: sewing methods have not
changed much over the years,
as can be seen in this photograph
of a flag-making shop at the
Brooklyn Navy Yard around the
time of World War I.*

3

THE FLAG
IN BATTLE

From the dawn of history, nations have carried their flags into battle. During the Crusades, or holy wars, soldiers often wore the emblems of their national patron saint on their cloaks. This practice encouraged them to sacrifice themselves for the honor of their country.

The practical uses of a flag in battle became evident very early. Flags could be seen from a distance, could identify the rank of a commander, and could indicate tactical maneuvers on the battlefield.

Flags have often been used to display the military power of a country. Victorious conquerors have taunted their enemies with captured flags, while dictators have used flags to mold public opinion. Whatever the cause, flags have inspired men and women to undertake dangerous military operations.

You have read about the growth of our flag, which parallels

the growth of our country. During this time the United States was sometimes involved in combat, both inside and outside its borders.

A CHRONOLOGICAL LIST OF CONFLICTS

War	Numbers of Stars in Flag
Revolutionary War (1775–1783)	13
War of 1812 (1812–1815)	15
Mexican War (1846–1848)	27, 28, 29
Civil War (1861–1865)	33, 34, 35, 36
Spanish-American War (1898)	45
World War I (1914–1918)	48
World War II (1939–1945)	48
Korean War (1950–1953)	48
Vietnam War (1961–1973)	50
Gulf War (1991)	50

For Americans, the flag has always carried multiple messages. Sometimes our flag has reinforced feelings of patriotism, and at other times it has represented opposition to war.

★ The Revolutionary War (1775–1781) ★

Many stories have been told about John Paul Jones, a Revolutionary War naval hero. One of the most famous concerns his exploits against the British on September 23, 1779. Jones, commander of the flagship *Bonhomme Richard*, fought against the British warship *Serapis*. When the *Bonhomme Richard* was close to sinking, the *Serapis* signaled, "Strike your colors." Jones replied, "I have not yet begun to fight."

After a brief battle, during which the *Bonhomme Richard* was sunk, the British surrendered to Jones and his men. Jones later supposedly wrote about this battle: "The very last vestige mortal eyes ever saw of the *Bonhomme Richard* was the defiant waving of her unconquered and unstricken Flag as she went down."

★ The Civil War (1861–1865) ★

Although many people wanted the national flag changed during the Civil War, President Abraham Lincoln rejected these proposals. During this troublesome period, the thirty-four-star flag was the one flown most extensively.

The Confederacy, not wishing to share a flag with the Union, adopted a flag of its own, the Stars and Bars. During the First Battle of Manassas (Bull Run) in July of 1861, the similarity of this flag to the Stars and Stripes created confusion on the battlefield.

To avoid such confusion in the future, the Confederate government established the Battle Flag in September of 1861. Also known as the Southern Cross, this flag became the most recognized symbol of the South.

*During a famous naval battle of the
Revolutionary War, John Paul Jones' flagship
Bonhomme Richard was sunk. The ship went
down with the tattered flag still flying.*

The Confederate flag was a symbol of the South during the Civil War. It is still flown in many areas of the South along with the Stars and Stripes.

★ World War I (1914–1918) and World War II (1939–1945) ★

The forty-eight-star flag, used longer than any other flag, represented our country in two of the worst conflicts the world has ever seen.

In 1917, the United States entered World War I, embarking on its first major overseas war. In this war 116,516 American soldiers were killed.

The forty-eight-star flag was flying over Pearl Harbor, Hawaii, on December 7, 1941, when the Japanese attacked the United States naval base. In response, the United States declared war on Japan, marking our entry into World War II.

★ The Vietnam War (1961–1973) ★

The fifty-star flag represented the United States in this conflict. Our country gradually drifted into this war, beginning in the early 1960s.

By the mid-1960s, we were involved in what had become the longest war in our history. Because the country was bitterly divided over the Vietnam War, the flag was often used as a tool of political dissent.

★ The Gulf War (1991) ★

In August 1990, Saddam Hussein, leader of Iraq, invaded the small neighboring country of Kuwait. Backed by United Nations resolutions condemning Hussein's actions, the United States and other countries joined forces and sent troops to the Persian Gulf.

*Top left: many flags were displayed at this Washington, D.C.,
victory parade for returning World War I troops.
Bottom left: a flag flies at the memorial at Pearl Harbor
in memory of those who died in the attack by the
Japanese on December 7, 1941. The memorial was built
over the sunken USS Arizona.
Above: at times the U.S. flag was worn as a form of
protest against the Vietnam War.*

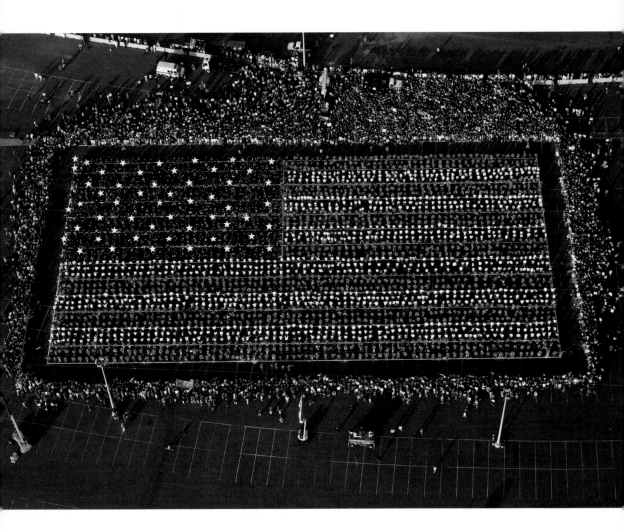

*Patriotism was at an all-time high during
the brief Persian Gulf War in early 1991.
Here several thousand people wearing red,
white, and blue T-shirts formed a giant
human flag to show support for U.S. troops.*

On January 17, 1991, the tense situation known as Desert Shield developed into a full-scale war called Desert Storm.

As public support for the war increased, Old Glory flew from homes, cars, and places of business. Players in various sports placed small flags on their helmets or uniforms. In San Diego, California, more than 3,600 people, wearing red, white, and blue T-shirts, formed a giant United States flag. New York City police deviated from a strict dress code and pinned flag patches on their uniforms. By the end of the brief war in February of 1991, the flag had become a very visible symbol of patriotism throughout America.

4
THE FLAG AND
THE ARTS

We Americans are proud of our flag. We salute it, pledge allegiance to it, and see it as a symbol of our diverse society. As a result of this intense feeling, the flag has repeatedly been used as a *motif*, or subject, in art, literature, and music to express feelings of patriotism and respect.

★ Art ★

From the early subdued paintings of the Revolution to the bright, garish colors of pop art, American artists have used the Stars and Stripes in their work. The red, white, and blue colors of Old Glory can be seen in everything from designs on inexpensive clothing to beautiful paintings that honor the flag.

John Trumbull (1756–1843)
This famous artist, who was an aide-de-camp to General Washington in the early days of the Revolution, painted some of the

most dramatic scenes of the war. Four of his paintings can be seen in the Rotunda of the United States Capitol in Washington, D.C.

In *The Death of General Warren*, Trumbull pictures a flag with a New England pine tree on its white canton, or top inner quarter. The pine tree was one of many regional symbols that replaced the British emblems on the flag.

Trumbull, who was called the pictorial recorder of the Revolution, also displays the flag in his work *The Capture of the Hessians at Trenton*. In 1776, George Washington took his army across the Delaware River into New Jersey to defeat a Hessian force of fifteen hundred men. In the painting, the battle is over. Both the living and the dead soldiers are shown, with the Grand Union flag in the center of the painting.

Frederick Childe Hassam (1859–1935)

During World War I, American painters often expressed their sentiments in patriotic pictures that showed the American flag. F. C. Hassam was one of the most famous in this group.

In Hassam's *The Avenue in the Rain* American flags dominate the painting, their colors deepened by the reflections on the wet pavement. Hassam pictured Fifth Avenue in New York City, which at that time was often hung with flags and patriotic banners.

On viewing Hassam's *The Fourth of July* one reviewer wrote that the painting "fairly shouts hurrah for Old Glory."

Jasper Johns (1930–   )

Jasper Johns, a major modern American artist, is famous for his paintings of the American flag. Known for his representation of

common objects, Johns calls attention to these objects and symbols through his art.

His paintings *Flag, 1954–1955* and *Flag on an Orange Field*, 1957, are from a series of flag paintings started in 1954.

★ Music ★

A naval bombardment during the War of 1812 inspired Francis Scott Key to compose in 1814 the words to the ''Star-Spangled Banner,'' the most famous tribute to the American flag. The song was first titled the ''Defence of Ft. McHenry'' and was sung to the music of ''To Anacreon in Heaven,'' a popular English song of that period. In 1931, the ''Star-Spangled Banner'' was officially adopted as the national anthem of the United States.

> Oh, say, can you see by the dawn's early light
> What so proudly we hailed at the twilight's last
>   gleaming?
> Whose broad stripes and bright stars through the
>   perilous fight
> O'er the ramparts we watched were so gallantly
>   streaming.
> And the rockets' red glare, the bombs bursting in
>   air

Famous artist Frederick Childe Hassam
depicted Allies Day, May 1917,
in this painting.

In 1814, during the War
of 1812, Francis Scott
Key (top) wrote the words
to the "Star-Spangled
Banner" while on board
a ship in Chesapeake Bay
off Baltimore (right).
The "Star-Spangled Banner"
was adopted as the U.S.
national anthem on
March 3, 1931.

Left: Flag on an Orange Field
is one of several paintings of the U.S.
flag by modern artist Jasper Johns.

Gave proof through the night that our flag was still
    there.
Oh, say, does that star-spangled banner yet wave
O'er the land of the free and the home of the
    brave?

George M. Cohan, a popular American composer, immortalized the flag in his composition "You're a Grand Old Flag."

You're a grand old flag, you're a high-flying flag
    And forever in peace may you wave.
You're the emblem of the land I love
    The home of the free and the brave. . . .

Cohan is also remembered for his patriotic musical comedies *Yankee Doodle Dandy* and *Over There*.

★ Poetry ★

On April 19, 1775, the opening battle of the Revolution was fought at the North Bridge, Concord, Massachusetts. Minutemen, volunteer groups of armed citizens, fought the British, who had attacked the villages of Concord and Lexington.

In commemoration of this event, the "Concord Hymn" was recited on July 4, 1837. Ralph Waldo Emerson, the American poet, wrote words which many students have memorized:

By the rude bridge that arched the flood,
    Their flag to April's breeze unfurled,
Here once the embattled farmers stood,
    And fired the shot heard round the world. . . .

*The writer Ralph Waldo Emerson wrote the "Concord Hymn,"
a poem about the first battle of the Revolution.*

In John Greenleaf Whittier's famous poem "Barbara Frietchie" (1864) the poet describes an incident that supposedly took place during the Civil War when Stonewall Jackson and his Confederate troops marched through Frederick, Maryland.

It was told that the only resident of the town to fly a Union flag was ninety-year-old Barbara Frietchie. As she waved it defiantly, she shouted,

"Shoot, if you must, this old gray head
But spare your country's flag. . . ."

5

THE FLAG AND THE CONSTITUTION

★ The Pledge of Allegiance ★

I pledge allegiance to the Flag of the United States of America and to the Republic for which it stands: one nation under God, indivisible, with liberty and justice for all.

Each school day, children all over the United States recite this pledge to the American flag. As with so many historical events surrounding our flag's history, the Pledge of Allegiance has been the focus of controversy since its conception. Court battles have been fought over the mandatory recitation of the pledge in schools, some parents insisting it is a loyalty oath that places an unnecessary burden on their children.

In 1892, *The Youth's Companion*, a weekly magazine for children, published the original version of the pledge as part of a

*Children reciting the Pledge of Allegiance in
an elementary school classroom*

promotional campaign for the four hundredth anniversary of Christopher Columbus's voyage to the New World in 1492. It was distributed in leaflet form to more than twelve million schoolchildren, who then recited it during the celebration.

Known as the "Youth Companion's Flag Pledge," the words read,

> I pledge allegiance to my flag and to the Republic for which it stands: one nation, indivisible, with liberty and justice for all.

Francis Bellamy has been recognized as the author even though his authorship was questioned for some time.

Over the years, changes have been made in the wording of the pledge. One June 14, 1923, representatives of the first National Flag Conference adopted a change, substituting the words "the flag of the United States of America" for "my flag." In 1954, Congress and President Dwight D. Eisenhower added the phrase "under God."

★ Supreme Court Decisions ★

Throughout our country's history some citizens, for one reason or another, have shown contempt for the flag. In the late 1800s, people were shocked to see the flag displayed in advertisements for whisky and chewing tobacco. A flag misuse bill was drafted but never reached the floors of Congress.

In 1897, patriotic societies formed the American Flag Association, declaring war on flag exploiters. At the same time, numerous states passed flag-desecration statutes, specifically banning advertisements showing the flag. Because of the flag desecration statutes, people have been prosecuted for wearing clothes patched with flags, flying a flag upside down, or using the flag as a decoration.

"Flag Salute" Case

In 1935, an intense legal battle was set in motion in Minersville, Pennsylvania. Members of Jehovah's Witnesses, a religious sect, objected on religious grounds to the mandatory recitation of the Pledge of Allegiance in public schools. As a result of their actions, all children who refused to salute the flag were expelled from school.

Between 1935 and 1940, there was an increase of public intolerance toward Jehovah's Witnesses. They were often forced to establish their own schools, and many members were jailed, beaten, and driven out of town. Others lost their jobs over the flag salute issue. On April 25, 1940, the "Flag Salute" case reached the Supreme Court, which upheld a state's right to impose the pledge.

Three years later, on June 14, 1943, the Court reversed its previous decision in the now famous case of *The West Virginia Board of Education* v. *Barnette*. Justice Robert H. Jackson wrote the majority opinion, which stated that the flag salute may not be made compulsory for any civilian. This decision stated that the rights of free conscience, guaranteed to the people by the Constitution, are rights superior to any right possessed by the government, state or federal.

First Amendment Rights

In 1984, during the Republican National Convention in Dallas, Texas, Gregory Lee Johnson, a member of the Revolutionary

Communist Youth Brigade, burned an American flag while a crowd yelled, "America, the red, white, and blue, we spit on you." Under Texas law, Johnson was sentenced to a year in jail and fined $2,000. Later, the Texas Criminal Appeals Court reversed this decision on constitutional grounds.

The Supreme Court was asked to reinstate the original conviction, but on June 21, 1989, by a vote of 5–4, the Court ruled that burning the American flag as a political protest was protected by the First Amendment's guarantee of free speech.

Public reaction to the decision was varied. Civil libertarians explained that people must be as free to burn the flag as to wave it, and that to jail people for expressive conduct is wrong. Veterans' groups immediately denounced the ruling on the grounds that this symbol of our nation should not be destroyed because too many lives have been sacrificed for it.

Numerous members of Congress demanded a constitutional amendment to protect the flag. In the absence of enough votes for an amendment, Congress passed the Flag Protection Act in October of 1989. This act made desecration of the flag punishable by up to one year in prison and a fine of as much as $1,000. Approved by both houses, the words "physically defiled" were added to the list of acts against the flag.

But this was not the end of the flag argument between the Supreme Court and Congress. On June 11, 1990, the Court threw out the Flag Protection Act, which had been adopted only nine months before. Justice William Brennan wrote that "punishing desecrators of the flag dilutes the very freedom that makes this emblem so revered, and worth revering."

On June 25, 1990, the Senate rejected another proposed constitutional amendment that would have permitted states to

Burning the American flag has become a form
of protest. The Supreme Court has ruled that the right
to burn the flag is protected by the First
Amendment's guarantee of free speech.
Right: two marchers in Washington, D.C. protest the
Supreme Court decision that flag burning is legal.

prosecute those who destroy or desecrate the American flag. The amendment, already defeated by the House of Representatives, lacked the necessary requirements to become law: approval by a two-thirds majority of the House and Senate, then ratification by thirty-eight states.

You have read about the historical development of the American flag and the controversies surrounding it from time to time. As future citizens you may or may not agree with the disputes, but one fact remains constant: the Stars and Stripes is the symbol of the principles we Americans believe in.

President Woodrow Wilson expressed his sentiments in 1917 when he said: "This flag, which we honor and under which we serve, is the emblem of our unity, our power, our thought and purpose as a nation. It has no character [other] than that which we give it from generation to generation. The choices are ours. . . ."

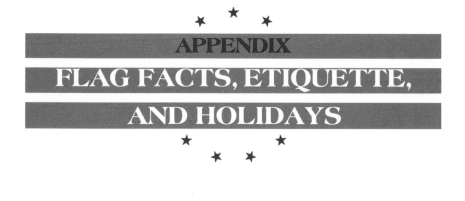

APPENDIX
FLAG FACTS, ETIQUETTE,
AND HOLIDAYS

★ Flag Facts ★

- The study of flag history is called *vexilology*.

- The original Stars and Stripes was first flown in the United States in 1777.

- The Bedford flag was the only banner carried by Americans on the first day of the Revolution.

- Many dry cleaners in the United States will clean an American flag free of charge.

- In 1835, William Driver, a sea captain, named the flag "Old Glory" when presented with one for his round-the-world trip.

- The United States Jack is a small flag usually flown from the bow of warships.

- The stars in our flag represent the fifty states collectively; no one star represents any particular state.

- Any person can write to his or her senators or representatives and for a reasonable fee (under $20) receive a piece of history—a flag that has "flown" over the United States Capitol building.

- During the Civil War, Thomas Custer, brother of General George Custer, was awarded two Medals of Honor for personally capturing two enemy flags.

★ Flag Etiquette ★

To supply a guide for the proper use and display of the flag, a Flag Code was drawn up at the National Flag Conference in 1923. The code was revised in 1924, and in June of 1942, Congress adopted a resolution that made the Flag Code a law. Some of the regulations are:

- The flag should be flown only from sunrise to sunset. When a patriotic effect is desired, it may be displayed twenty-four hours a day if properly illuminated during the hours of darkness.

- The flag should be hoisted briskly and lowered ceremoniously.

- The flag should not be displayed on days when the weather is bad, except when an all-weather flag is displayed.

- The flag should be displayed on or near the main administration building of every public institution.

- The flag should be displayed in or near every polling place on election day.

- The flag should be displayed during the school day in or near every schoolhouse.

That no disrespect should be shown to the flag of the United States of America:

- The flag should not be dipped to any person or thing.

- The flag should never be displayed with the union, the section containing the stars, down, except as a signal of dire distress.

- The flag should never touch anything beneath it.

- The flag should never be carried flat or horizontally, but always aloft and free.

- The flag should never be used as wearing apparel.

- The flag should never be used for advertising purposes.

- No part of the flag should ever be used as a costume or athletic wear.

- A flag in unsuitable condition should be destroyed in a dignified manner.

The flag should be displayed on all days, but especially on:

New Year's Day (January 1)

Inauguration Day (January 20)

Presidents' Day (third Monday in February)

Easter Sunday (date varies)

Mother's Day (second Sunday in May)

Armed Forces' Day (third Saturday in May)

Memorial Day (half staff until noon, the last Monday in May)

Flag Day (June 14)

Independence Day (July 4)

Labor Day (first Monday in September)

Constitution Day (September 17)

Columbus Day (second Monday in October)

Navy Day (October 27)

Veterans' Day (November 11)

Thanksgiving Day (fourth Thursday in November)

Christmas Day (December 25)

To view the original Star-Spangled Banner, which Francis Scott Key memorialized in our national anthem, visit the:

National Museum of American History
14th St. & Constitution Avenue NW
Washington, DC 20002

The flag is on display about seven times a day on the half hour. At that time, the linen cover that protects it is withdrawn and visitors can view the original flag. A special program provides background facts about the flag. For further information call the Smithsonian Information Center (202) 357-2700.

For information about the United States flag, you can write to:

The Flag Research Center
3 Edgehill Road
Winchester, MA 01890

U.S. Capitol Historical Society
200 Maryland Ave. NE
Washington, DC 20002

Veterans of Foreign Wars
National Dept. of Americanism
34th & Broadway
Kansas City, MO 64111

FOR FURTHER READING

Crampton, William, *Flag*. New York: Knopf, 1989.

Crouthers, David D. *Flags of American History*. Maplewood, NJ: Hammond Incorporated, 1973.

Dupuy, Trevor, ed. *Holidays*. New York: Franklin Watts, 1965.

Mayer, Albert, *The Story of Old Glory*. Chicago: Children's Press, 1970.

Parrish, Thomas, *The American Flag*. New York: Simon and Schuster, 1973.

Smith, Whitney, *American Flags from Washington to Lincoln*. Santa Barbara, CA: Bellerophon Books, 1990.

Williams, Earl P. *What You Should Know About the Flag*. Lanham, MD: Maryland Historical Press, 1987.

INDEX

ABOUT THE AUTHOR

Ann Armbruster has been an English teacher and a school librarian. Her career as a librarian inspired her to write books and articles for young people.

Another of her books for Watts, written in collaboration with Elizabeth A. Taylor, is *Astronaut Training*.

Ann Armbruster lives in Ohio, where she pursues her interest in history.